IF YOUR MAN AIN'T SHIT, READ THIS

The Mind Set

Published by FastPencil Publishing

IF YOUR MAN AIN'T SHIT, READ THIS

First Edition

Print edition ISBN: 9781495831126

Copyright © The Mind Set 2022

All rights reserved. No part of this publication may be reproduced, stored in a retrieval system, or transmitted, in any form, or by any means, electronic, mechanical, photocopying, recording, or otherwise, without the prior consent of the publisher.

Sale of this book without a front cover may be unauthorized. If the book is coverless, it may have been reported to the publisher as "unsold or destroyed" and neither the author nor the publisher may have received payment for it.

http://www.fastpencil.com

Printed in the United States of America

Table of Contents

Chapter 1 If Your Man Ain't Shit, Read This 13

Chapter 2 Symptoms of Mr. Ain't Shit 15

Chapter 3 If He Cheats 23

Chapter 4 If He Stays Out Late/ If He Doesn't Take You Out (Anymore) 31

Chapter 5 If He Shuts Down When the Convo Is Real 39

Chapter 6 If the Marriage Convo Is One that He Often Neglects 45

Chapter 7 If He Talks to You in a Demeaning Manner 51

Chapter 8 Doesn't Treat You as an Equal 57

Chapter 9 If He Hits You – RUN! 63

Chapter 10 The Solution 69

I'd like to dedicate this work to my first teacher on all concerning

life. The source of my ambition and stubborn ways is my mother, Eva Jones

ACKNOWLEDGEMENTS:

This journey has been more than words can express. To be reading these words, is to be smack dab in the middle of conversations that I've had with some of my closest friends, male and female. To now see my mind frame and thoughts manifested in this form and shared with the world, is a dream come true.

Especially coming from a place where dreams turn into nightmares vary fast (a prison cell). It was truly during my darkest moment when the universe introduced me to my greatest gift this writing thing.

A mix of strong support and a crowd of haters that wanted to see men fall is the recipe for this genius mind and this million dollar grind. I want to first give thanks to the universe (GOD) for EVERYTHING AND EVERYBODY, even the ones that are no longer here. I want to thank my Mother Eva, (SHAY) for always giving me the unadulterated truth, even at times when I didn't want to hear it. My step father Larry (PJ) for being what she needed when she needed him the most, I salute you a 100xs over King.

I want to thank my son Nasaun, (TRAY) and my one and only brother Steven (BUDDY)

for still looking up to me and holding me in high reguards reguardless of circumstances,

unconditional love is what they've taught me.

I wanna thank my extended family (the family that I've made)

Lamontay Young (Big Tay) for showing me the ropes when no one else could.

Dontae Ward, for standing shoulder to shoulder with me as I turned the things that we thought into reality.

Antonio Corprew (Tone-Tone) the first one to let me know I was made to be a "BOSS"

Keontae Saunders, truly my lil bro.

My man BIG (BIGGMONEYPERIOD) for standing firm and being the true definition of solid.

My lil partner "YAK" hard headed as hell but still my man nevertheless, I know I be down on you but I just want the best for you.

My man Deezy, one of the first to let me know that I might really have a future in this writing thing.
And last but no least, my loving wife....

(I don't have a wife, but if I did I'm pretty sure that I'd say something like..)
I'd like to thank you baby for ALWAYS holding me down, even when you didn't agree with some of my wild decisions. Thank you truly the entire world was against me and I was being crucified from every angle. I'm a big deal by myself but together we're a problem.

You made me realize that this game of life is a team game.

Truly my motivation to be the best version of myself at all times.

She'd love to read that about herself right?

Before I close for good, I give my final thanks to everyone who gave up on me and counted me out.

Nothing motivated and fires me more than knowing that I'm doing what was deemed impossible, **STILL LIVING!!!!!**

Chapter 1 If Your Man Ain't Shit, Read This

If you're reading these words right now, that's a clear indication that you're in a relationship that's rocky and you're seriously considering pulling the plug or you're in a relationship that's rocky and you have hopes of salvaging it. Either way I'm here to give you a definitive guide to help you make that decision. First and foremost, this information comes from a man that has either been in the same shoes as the very one you're dealing with right now or has had a friend or two that matches the description to a tee.

Through my own travels, as I now reflect on some of my fondest relationships mishaps, I'm conscious of the fact that a lot of my reactions were a result of preceding ACTIONS of my lover, and yes, I did say that correctly. Now, I know that to you, that one statement may sound like bullshit. It probably really sounds like bullshit when I say that the problem may not be him at all and, that it might be you, but, but, but... before you throw this great book in the garbage or fireplace, please keep an open mind because if so, I guarantee you will make the very best decision regarding your relationship.

Up until this point, I know that you've probably already figured out that we (men) at times aren't the best of communicators. And if you feel this way, you're 100 percent correct. But, that's just the way we're wired, which leads to a lack of understanding and pure chaos. But right here and right now, we're here to address some of your main concerns plus more. In this book, I plan to outline and give you a better understanding of the following: Why he lies, why he cheats, why he stays out late, why he shuts down when the convo gets real, why the marriage convo is one that he often neglects, why he talks to you in a demeaning manner, why he doesn't treat you as an equal, and such.

I promise you, by the last chapter of this book, you will know for certain what you should do. Without further ado, let's start at the very beginning.

Chapter 2 Symptoms of Mr. Ain't Shit

Let's start off with the person in question right now, Mr. Ain't Shit. First and foremost, I want it to be very clearly understood that Mr. Ain't Shit comes in two different forms:
 Mr. Ain't-Shit-But-Can-Be and
 Mr. Ain't-Shit-and-Ain't-Gonna-Be.

To the naked eye, they look identical. They do some of the same dumb shit, walk the same, and may even talk the same, but when you scratch the surface, they are built completely different.

First, we'll start off with Mr. Ain't-Shit-But-Can-Be. Attractive, ain't he? Fly? Good sex? But that's where the good shit ends. To the core, he's a liar, he's a cheater, and every other thing that you an most of your home girls talk about over vodka-laced conversations and tears. Nine times out of ten, he's done shit that you probably should've left for years ago (if it's been that long), but there's something in him, that you and only you see that keeps you holding on to this person that everyone that deals with you hates.

Well, I got good news. Although he may be a stinking piece of shit, he may be saved. How? You're probably asking because you've cried and fought'em so much that it seems to be no avail.

Ladies, the problem in this type of man is not him at all. It's not? No, it's you!

Now before you say fuck me and throw this amazing book in your fireplace, please read on because this stinking piece of shit that you love sooooooo much, we can save him. Believe it or not, he needs you just as much as you may feel that you need him. Trust me.

By the way, we will call Mr. Ain't-Shit-but-Can-Be... Trey! Yeah, I like Trey. It's gotta "he ain't shit but can be" ring to it, doesn't it? See, Trey isn't bad by virtue; or even has moral-compass issues. Trey is affected by your very own "manufactured" bullshit, and just like a compromise with this man, but we'll delve into this deeper real soon.

Then we have Mr. Ain't-Shit-and-Ain't-Gonna-Be. Now out of the two, this character is the one that is not going to take too much explaining to describe or decipher because his "bullshit" is so blatant that a blind person can see it.

These are the guys that only mama should love (his mama). These guys are what I call, "for no reason" guys, meaning that they do shit for no good reason. They don't even have to be provoked to do some dumb shit. I personally despise this character so much simply because during my own "ain't shit" days, I would commonly be mistaken for him and missed out on some real... prime opportunities, for a lack of better words, simply because he came just like me on the surface.

CHAPTER 2 SYMPTOMS OF MR. AIN'T SHIT

Ladies this man (Mr. Ain't-Shit-and-Ain't-Gonna-Be) can never trusted, kept, habilitated, worked on, or worked out. He's just not built for it. At best, he's simply good for the moment. He's rotten to the core and CANNOT BE SAVED. Meet, Dion!

Dion is the one that links you in through your insecurities and intends to keep you in a fucked-up head space because the more off-balanced you are with your thinking, the more of a hold he keeps over you. Dion is the one that uses your house as a secure spot to stay, he uses you, pays little to no bills, has nothing to offer you, will fuck anything moving, and cats up all the kids' snacks. Dion is TROUBLE big-time and will always be.

In this book, not only am I going to give you the outlook, perspective, and movements of both Trey (can be saved) and Dion (can't be saved), but I'm also going to give you the movements of two different types of women that either contribute to the actions of these men or motivate the actions. If everything that I say about Dion sounds just like the trash that's drunk and asleep right now on your couch due to some recent dumb shit that he's done, with an empty condom wrapper in his pocket, then you will pinpoint him and deal with him accordingly. It's gonna be long bumpy ride, but I promise you that; as long as you don't prematurely abort, we'll get there together, and in better shape than ever before.

Ready? It's causal Saturday night, and Trey is in the shower getting ready for the night out with the fellas. You come into the bedroom and see a brand-new outfit laid out, and a fly pair of shoes to match. You also notice a fresh bottle of cologne that must be new too because you're not familiar with it. Smells good though.

His phone vibrates on the dresser. Without thinking twice, you go over to pick it up and see that it's a text message that reads: "Already lit! We can't wait to see you tonight, my dude."

Before you put the phone down, you casually scroll through all of his other text messages just to see who he has been talking to. Nothing really catches your eyes. You put the phone back down just as he's making his exit from the bathroom. As he's getting dressed, you ask him a million-and-one questions about the night. "Who's going to be there tonight?", "Will any women be there", you ask. This is the only thing that you're worried about due to the fact that Trey already has a slip-up or two on his resume. He exhales deeply and tells you, no. He leaves. You're home. Mind is wondering now about various things. You send him a text, one that says, "I hope you're having fun." He replies, "I am." The night goes by, and he walks in about two in the morning.

You awake the next morning bright and early to go and wash clothes. At the Laundromat, you ran into the girlfriend of the friend's party that it was. She asks you why you didn't come. It wasn't a total boy's night. It was a mixed crowd, meaning that other women were there. Your mind goes into overdrive. You rush back home; you can't wait to see Trey because you're gonna lay his lying ass out.

You walk in and go ape-shit. What has you most upset is not the fact that he didn't invite you but the fact that he told you that there weren't going to be any other women there.

Real talk... Now, ladies, I want you to be honest for a second. Is the woman in this scenario you? Are you feeling like; "Why didn't he just tell me the truth? Why didn't he invite me?" This just reaffirms that Trey is a lying piece of shit, right? WRONG, and let me tell you why. Dealing with you for the length of time that Trey has, he knows what he's dealing with. And what he's dealing with is an insecure woman that doesn't trust him as far as her eyes can see him. Your insecurities make you see the very worst in every situation and question everything he does.

Did Trey know that there were going to be other women there? You damn right he did. "Well, why didn't he tell me the truth?" you ask.

BECAUSE YOU MAKE IT HARD TO TELL YOU THE TRUTH! Yeah, yeah, I know you're cursing me out right now, nut putting all bullshit to the side, you know that this is the truth. He had told you yes, there would've been a thousand more questions behind the initial thousand that you asked, leading up to that one. Ladies, don't make it hard for us to tell you the truth and then get mad when we lie. No man wants to be condemned as if he's done something wrong simply because he told you the truth about something that he was innocent on. If you're going to go crazy every time you hear something unfavorable, don't be surprised that you have a man that will never tell you the truth about small things THAT HE SHOULD BE ABLE TO TELL YOU THETRUTH ABOUT. Simple!

Then you say, "Well, why didn't he invite me? All of the other ladies were there?" "He was probably talking to other women with his slick ass."

Well, first of all, he didn't invite you for the same reasons that he lied to you about the other women being there. You would've acted like a damn fool! Remember earlier when I said that your insecurities make you see shit that isn't even there? This would've been one of those moments. Just thinking that he's an untamed dog, every attractive woman that you see, you just know that he's looking at. And Lord forbid that he takes part in an innocent conversation or joke that involves another woman; that man might just lose his life that night because you're going to swear that he has talked to "all types of fuck ups." So to ensure that he had a good night, he left your ass right at home.

Ladies, in addition to not wanting to be condemned for telling the truth, we also don't want to have to walk on eggshells with you simply because any and everything offends you, especially anything dealing with another female. The strongest quality that a woman can display is confidence, and that's universal.

All in all, if Trey lies, it's simply because YOU DON'T MAKE IT EASY FOR HIM TO DO ANYTHING BUT LIE. Now I'm not saying it's right or justified, but I am giving you a reason.

Now let's flip the coin for a second. The woman this time isn't one that's lead by her insecurities or one that condemns one for telling the truth. On the contrary, she's a very rational and logical one al-

Chapter 2 Symptoms of Mr. Ain't Shit

though she has every reason to be an insecure snooper.

Dion scenario. There's no specific scenario for a Dion. Dion will lie about every damn thing just because. Dion will tell you the sky is red just for the gratification for deceiving you. Hell, his name might not even be Dion for all we know. Dion isn't meant to be a permanent situation; he knows this, which is why none of his lies are calculated regardless of what he does and how much he lies, you will accept him and all of his shit. I mean, think about it for a second, If there are no consequences for his acting out, why would he stop? Why would he think twice?

Whereas, Trey lies because of fear of the consequences of the truth, Dion is just a "damn liar".

We all know people like this. People that just makes you say, "He/she is a lying mutha------." This is Dion. He has no moral compass, and this identifies his character to the core. In conclusion, I leave you with this: Unless you're a psycho or a Dion, nobody "likes to lie". In general (with the exception of psychos and Dion), the reason that people lie is because they either flat out fear the consequences of the truth or are trying to delay the consequences of the truth. In the event that you're dealing with a Trey, someone that can be saved, don't make it hard for him to tell you the truth.

If you are willing to continue to deal with him, don't allow the past to dictate how you deal with him, and that's your past and his.

Which brings me to a subject of great concern for a second. Ladies, if you feel that you positively can't get over something that he's done, LET HIM GO. For you to feel that way, that means that he's done something so malicious that this relationship is irreparable. Now, I'm not going to classify what's "so malicious" to you; because only you can define that, but I will say, of there is something that has taken place that you just cannot let go, end the relationship.

Whether you want to face it now or later, your inability to forgive this man will inevitably end this relationship anyway, and the longer you hold on with these feelings, the worse the relationship will get because the more you're disconnected, the less of a "good woman" you can be for him, which will cause him to continue to do dumb shit, thus setting y'all back further and further.

Now back to the regularly scheduled program... Had you not been so crazy acting, he would've gladly told you that other women were going to be there. Hell, he might've even invited you to come along, and who knows, y'all might've had a great night together. On the flip, there's nothing that you could've done to prevent Dion from lying to you! NOTHING! And being the good sane woman that you are, had there been parameters set in the beginning you wouldn't be reading these words right now, trying to figure out if Dion is worth the rest of you time. Trey was caught in a catch-22, and Dion... well, Dion was just being Dion.

Chapter 3 If He Cheats

Now being the avid book reader that I am, I know for a fact that some of you skipped straight to this part. If so, I am not going to hold it against you, I promise Due to the fact that no two women are the same, I know that the parameters of cheating varies slightly, But for this chapter, we're going to define cheating as "any illegitimate action with someone else that isn't you intended spouse." Who am I kidding? We're talking about him having sex with other women, right? There are so many factors that can lead a decent man to cheat, and that will be what we will focus on first. Now I know that I will have a fair share of women say, "I can't MAKE him do anything," but I strongly disagree. Ladies, a lot of times, infidelity on our behalf stems from a lack of simple things (love, drive communication, food, sex, and good sex) and too much of the frivolous shit (complaining, arguing, laziness, dependability,a lack of understanding, unwillingness to compromise, or a combination of them all). We all know that a relationship is comprised of a lot of elements. I look at it like a car; To keep it in driving condition, you must keep up the maintenance. It's the same way in a relationship. Your trust, mental stimulation (another biggie), confidence, and lastly love.

Let me give you a breakdown of this relationship vehicle really quick. We'll first start with communication. Communication is the motor of this whole thing. I can't stress how much important it is to birth a healthy line of communication and maintain it. Considering that you're reading this right now, it's a good chance that on a scale of 1 to 10, the communication in your relationship is between a 1 to 3.

A lot of people confuse communication with a lot of talking. That's not communication. That's talking. Communicating is when you're able to exchange EFFECTIVELY. Communication doesn't mean that you're always right, but it ensures that you always get results. Communication means that we ALWAYS know where one another is coming from, leaving no one misunderstood.

Next, it's trust, the tires. It's hard to be led by someone that you can't/ don't trust and harder to lead someone who doesn't trust you. Simply put, without it, your relationship will inevitably be in the same shape as trying to drive a car with only wheels on it, going nowhere fast, and it's going to cost you a lot along the way. Although communication is the most important, mental stimulation, "Windows", is my favorite by far. Ladies, as your man, in addition to stimulating your body, it should be a must that I stimulate your mind, and I'm not just speaking sexually. I should challenge you to be your absolute best version of yourself. I should not only motivate you but also push you past your self-imposed limitations that you've put on yourself. I should be able to effectively communicate with you on an array of subjects, always leaving you with a new state of clarity on something that you didn't perceive that way before.

The true meaning of building and not destroying. I call it "Windows" because just like the glass that protect us against debris and elements, mental stimulation protects us from stagnation. Okay, let's be real for a second. How many have you had that came like that? Okay, back to business.

We've now arrived at the seatbelts, confidence. Confidence is a rarity nowadays, and by confidence, I mean, KNOWING, sureness. As your man, you should, without a doubt, know your place in my life. The lack of this knowing is the catalyst to insecurities, and as we both witnessed in the first chapter, insecurities tend to make an unsteady situation turbulent. I call it the "seatbelts" because the "seatbelts" are the only thing in the car that truly keeps you secured in your spot.

Lastly, it's love; that serves as the "body of the car". We all know that the body isn't the most important part but often the most attractive part. Some may not agree, but love alone is far from enough to sustain any healthy relationship.

Without the first four components, the love that you have for a person will always be just a feeling. The greatest misconception of love is that it's enough. And that misconception has been the reason that so many have endured, held on, and refuse to let go when that was the best thing to do. It's a new age. Love is far from enough.

Now that we understand what a healthy relationship is comprised of, I'm going to show you how those same elements can be the catalyst to Mr. "Ain't Shit."

If he cheats… it could be because you make it hard for him to keep up the maintenance. Are you the woman that is hard to communicate with because you always have to be right? When angered, do you turn into a poor listener? Do you often yell as if that makes your point come across quicker?

Ladies, we need you to be our lover, not a second mother. No man wants a woman that he can't talk to or one that refuses to listen. To be able to lay down and effectively discuss ANYTHING (that is, good things or bad things), is a breath of fresh air and could be one of the reasons that he slept with such and such from up the street. Do you make it hard to trust him? Are you so stuck in the past (your past and, his past) that you refuse to give him a little rope for fear that he can't control himself? Big mistake!

As we discussed in the lying chapter, that super suspicious shit gets played out real fast. The last thing that you want is for him to feel like, "She already believes that I'm up to no good, so I might as well."

Ladies, if your man ever adopts this line of thinking, your ass is in trouble. Trust me on that if you trust nothing else. If you're all burnt out on trust, let him go while y'all are still on good terms because if not, you'll probably end up hating him.

Do you fight the mental stimulation? Do you lack ambition and drive? Ladies, if you have a man that's capable of mental stimulation, consider yourself lucky. The man that is capable, though, finds it a major turnoff when what he's giving is not being received in the ways that they should. No man desires a lazy woman, and just because you have a job doesn't mean that you aren't lazy (because I know that you were about to go there). For the "go-getter" type of man, the boss type, nothing is more attractive than the woman that's either also bossed up or willing to be bossed up. So when you catch him dealing with a woman that's in a better position that you, he didn't choose or cheat with her because she has more than you. It's because she's willing to do something that you aren't. Level up. This may be the area that you really need to reflect on because this area could be the reason that you no longer have a man. Fuck cheating. He's gone altogether! Are you steady on the fence about where you stand in his life? Do you make it hard to love you like you "feel" you should be?

We know that women will be women, but we hate that hot-and-cold shit. We hate it when one day, you know that you're number one in my life, and the next day, you don't know your place. We hate it when you wear your insecurities on your sleeve especially for no good reason. A big part of confidence comes from you knowing your own self-worth. When you definitively know your worth, it shows on you unconsciously. When you know your self-worth, it translates as, "I don't worry about him fucking up because he knows what he has, and if he doesn't, he will when

I'm gone." That's you living fully in your worth. Insecurities are negative emotions, and a law of nature states that like begets like, So, entertaining of one negative emotions; births others just like it, and before you know it, you've turned into a black cloud to be around. And who likes to be around that?

Which walks right into the love comporting. A combination of these things makes it hard for me to love you in full capacity. If I can barely stand to be around you or cringe at the thought of talking to you, then how can my love for you be fully manifested? The lack of love at home makes it easy to find it elsewhere. If the love at home is over the top, there is no room for it to flourish from anywhere else.

Sex! Before ending this chapter, it's a must that I briefly skim the surface on the topic of sex. This is by far one of the most important areas to pay attention to when cheating is the topic. Ladies, we are sexual beings and primitive as hell when it comes to getting busy. Shallow? Maybe, but this is who we are. And it shows in our actions. What do you think is the motivation behind nice cars, big rims, jewelry, and fly gear? It's not for the sake of blowing money. No, for most of us, these things are done (or done to the extreme) with thoughts of pussy in mind. So, if a man is willing to go this far to elevate his pussy rate, then you know that we have little-to-no understanding when our woman isn't putting out. (Now, please understand that I'm not speaking for the "excessive freaks" that seem to need it SIX-TO-SEVEN times a day.) Through sex is how we express ourselves and being frank about it, we need a healthy dose of it. We don't want to have to schedule sexual sessions like it's a workout, and we don't have to beg you for it either. And I know that some of you may say, "Well, Trey isn't that good at it, so I don't really like it all of the time, "But have you ever stopped to think that he may not be good at it because you don't give him enough practice? You laugh, but I'm serious. Ladies, sometimes, it takes for you to take your man to school to make him that world-class lover. We're wired different. We tend to think that, the same way the last one liked it, this one will too. If we're not hitting it right, teach us. Don't hold the pussy hostage and make me have a standoff for it. That's a sure way to send him around the corner.

And another thing, you can't just "give it up", Sometimes, you have to rock his socks. I'm talking about that "mind-blowing and, toes-curling, shake when it's finished" type of sex. Every man is fool for a "freak". You' don't have to be her every day, all week, but you must let us know that she's there. And the she that I speak of, is her that drops down when he least expects it and gives up an oral clinic that makes him call on GOD! Ladies, I would bet money that; the very next time you see your man, before you say one word to him, you drop down and put on that clinic. With that, you change the outcome of the entire day. You caught him so off guard that, you might fuck around and get a car today!

In conclusion, everything that was just outlined is from the mind of a Trey. He's not the low-down cheating-ass dog that you and your home girls have him pegged as. You just put him in precarious positions.

Now Dion, on the other hand, is a different story all together. Once again, let's say that you aren't the "crazy" insecure woman that's withholding sex as his capital punishment. Let's say that you are the sound listener and, excellent communicator that's just a ball of love, waiting on her knight and shining armor to boss her up. Dion will see none of this, and if he does, he won't even know what it is that he's looking at Mental stimulation?

What? Dion is incapable of upgrading, bossing up, or leading you anywhere. Remember, he's eating the kids' snacks. The only thing that he's good for is good sex. Dion usually well equipped and knows how to use it, he has to, and he has nothing else to offer.

DO NOT BE DICK DUMB! I REPEAT,DO NOT BE DICK DUMB! He's going to cheat regardless of what you do or how well you do it. Once again, HE CAN'T BE SAVED!

Chapter 4 If He Stays Out Late/ If He Doesn't Take You Out (Anymore)

How many nights have you sat up wondering exactly how long he will stay out without calling you? More times than you can count, I bet. And when he keeps these long hours, are these some of the thoughts that creep in your mind? "Where is he? I bet he's doing something that he doesn't have any business doing." Or "I know he's with (suspected her)."

These are the thoughts, right? Well, what if you found out that he wasn't doing anything wrong at all, and he just didn't want to be around you? You may then say, "Well, he knows that it irks me to my core when he keeps late hours, and what type of man with a woman stays out all night anyway?" I'ma tell you right now what kind of man stays out all night, the man doesn't want to be bothered with your bullshit tonight, or last night, or most nights for that matter. Ladies, although this is chapter 4, this sign may be precursor to the first three chapters. No man, or nobody (with some damn sense) wants to be trapped in a house with someone that's just a negative ball of energy. What's negative energy? I'm glad you asked. It is complaining about everything, nitpicking about the smallest of things, or when you get in your funny acting ways and don't want him to touch you, hug you, or even say anything to you, (and y'all know y'all do this). You didn't cook anything because you still tudin over some shit that took place a week ago that probably wasn't even that serious. So in addition to my man Trey being at work all day, and chasin' the bag, he also has to come home and cook his own food. And 9 times out of 10, if he wants to get his shit off (have sex and catch a decent nut), he's gonna have to break down put the lotion on because you've slightly waged war and are adamant about givin' him no ass.

With that being said, would you be in a rush to come home to this? Hell no! Ladies, please understand that; home is our safe zone. It's our place of serenity. Home is the place where we feel that we're supposed to be able to let our hair down, kick off the shoes, and leave the stressors of the world at the free zone. We're supposed to look forward to coming home because, for one, I just know that my queen is there waiting on me with some good love and affection, and I'm not necessarily talking about sexing. No, good love and affection can come in the form of me just holding you, rubbing your feet/ you rubbing mine as we exchange each other's day, or just laying up being cool. Good love can be massaging my back in an attempt to ease my mind. Things like these make me want to come home for more than sleep and to change clothes.

Please understand that we're not asking you to put your hard hat and be superwoman after a long day that you may have had yourself, but we're not looking forward to walking into another war zone; one that's potentially worse, after leaving the one that the world has to offer.

Now I know that by this point, I've accumulated my faire share of debates that are probably going to ask something like. "Well, what about when I've had a long day?", or "What about when I need the house to be my serenity"? Rightfully so, you're justified in asking that. This relationship thing is a two-way street. We don't mind being that for you, and in the case of Treys, I think we show that by NEVER COMING WITH THE SAME SHIT YOU COME WITH. We don't mind being your calm after the storm, ladies, but allow us to be that.

Don't take the bullshit that the world has given you and project it off on us. Hell, we didn't do it. It's simple as giving your man a heads-up, "Listen, baby, the day has been a long bad one..." Just that statement alone let's me know that I have to help you hit a positive reset, even if my own day was trash. We might have to sit face-to-face, rubbing each other's feet and, talking about how the world has us both "fucked-up". As much as you all will like us to be, most of us aren't automatic. Especially if you have this "crazy" shit going on, we don't know if you had a bad day or you're just in one of your fucked-up moods. COMMUNICATE things with us. Teach us. A lot of us don't know off the bat how to be the "ideal lover" for you, but we can be that if you will simply show us. We're (most men) not like that purposely, but you have to understand that these things come with experience. So even though one may have been with numerous women before you, how many of them has showed him the ropes on exactly how he has to treat a WOMAN? I'm not saying that you have to raise a man, but you may definitely have to CULTIVATE him.

Trey doesn't want to run away from you, and he doesn't have intentions of disrespecting the fact that you'd like him home at a decent hour, but he also doesn't want to walk into the crossfire of this crazy person's shit that you have going on either. So as you can see, you've literally put him between a rock and a hard place. Contrary to what you may believe, we feel.

Now Dion, on the other hand, has an entire other angle that he's coming from. In addition to all of the bullshit that he already has going on and has you going through, he also keeps long hours and sometimes doesn't come home period. Dealing with Dion, this probably has nothing at all to do with you, because you cook frequently and, keep a clean house, sex isn't an issue (because remember, sex with Dion's most pleasurable, and that's all he has to offer), and you don't really nag and, complain (simply because you don't require too much from him).

"So why the long hours?" you asking, right? Simply put, Dion does what he does as a show that no one woman can control him. Dion is a true rebel to any and all systems that ANY woman puts into place. You can talk to him about it, argue with him, fight him, whatever. He'll never change, which is the differentiating factor between him and Trey.

After some minor adjustments, Trey will be what you want and, what you need. With Dion, no matter what you do, his lack of overall respect for women in general will never allow him to succumb to something as small as a curfew. In his mind, he feel like, " She got me fucked up if she thinks she can run me". Boundaries, ladies, boundaries! Had you paid attention to the "essentials" instead of the smokescreen shit (good sex, good looks, security, etc.), Dion wouldn't have you all stressed out right now; but we can't cry over spilled milk. Just read on, I'ma get you through it.

He Doesn't Take You Out Anymore. When you first met Trey, did he woo you by taking you out every chance that you'd allow him to? Did he charm you by looking into your eyes and pouring out his heart, making your very own melt? Even when y'all first moved in together, did he still go out of his way to take you out? So, what changed, you ask? If I had guess, the same reasons that he stays out late probably the same reasons that he doesn't want to take you anywhere. Ladies, when we take you out, it's served as a double purpose. First, it's because we just love to see you happy and love the fact that we're the reason for your smile. We love being around you. Second, it's to show my queen off to the world. You are my trophy. You represent the fact that "hey, I've done something right, and the universe has seen fit to reward me with this amazing woman." Y'all know we love to show off, so any chance we get, we want the world to see exactly how God has blessed us. So, in the event that you have made the relationship toxic, or are making it toxic, you're lowering the threshold for what we can stand until we eventually get to the point where we no longer feel that "show off" way about you anymore. After so many instances of you accusing him of flirting with the waitress, or cutting his eyes at the woman with the big ass that just walked past, or simply just acting in a negative way, do you really wonder why he takes you nowhere, or has not even thought about it? If we guaranteed to get a headache at home, we don't need to take the show on the road. Ladies, don't make it hard for Trey!

As always, the Dion situation seems similar but is comprised of completely different elements. I can almost bet that every time you and Dion went out, it was at you request and probably at your expense, right? Why? I'll give you two reasons: (1) His ass doesn't have any money, or (2) he doesn't see you enough value to wine and dine you like you should be wined and dined. One thing is for sure, you always know the things that a man values, simply by what he spends most of his resources on (weed, shoes, his car, his gear, etc.) If you aren't part of the equation, then it's good chance that you don't mean shit to him, and I'm just being frank about it. How many times has he gotten your hair done, paid for a spa day, gotten your nails and feet done, purchased you some gear? See what I mean? It's been all you, ain't it? Dion is what you'd call a human leach. He's there for something more than you and your company. You offer him security in other areas, allowing him to leach off of you. Once again, the focus goes back to parameters and boundaries, ladies. Had this been set from the beginning, you wouldn't be trying to filter him now; he would've filtered himself. Most of us will only do what you make us do. If you make us do nothing, we'll do just that, NOTHING!

Chapter 5 If He Shuts Down When the Convo Is Real

That's right. This is the one you want right here, ain't it? This is by far one of the most talked about topics that I've heard women speak of over and over again.

"How come every time we start talking about feelings, he just shuts down and look stupid?" or "Why doesn't he ever say much when I talk about how he neglects me or makes me feel?"

This topic is spin-off of what we briefly discussed about communication. Ladies, unless you're just dealing with a primitive dumbass that's incapable of giving you feedback, there's absolutely nothing wrong with our faculties.

When Trey shuts down, it's simply because he knows that this is the best thing for him to do. If not, it's a good chance that a straight-up "Real Talk" conversation will turn into a verbal sparring session or, worse, a real live WWE wrestling match.

Ladies, you often say that you want the truth. You often ask for the truth, but, the truth of the matter is, that's not what you want at all. I know you're probably saying, "How do you sound? What else do I want?" Answer this: If Trey told you, "I have been keeping long hours because I just can't stand to be around your ass." How would you take it? See what I mean? By this point of relationship, you have Trey feeling so many ways about so many different things that if he was to start with you on "expression tour", as I like to call it, he'll probably be dead before he can even finish.

It's always a plus to deal with someone that's an extrovert, but a woman that's a good listener, has the secret key to any man's heart. Most just don't know it. It's human nature to try to find fault or point out the fault in others when there is smoke in the city, but for a relationship, that could be the linchpin to the ticking time bomb. Ladies, nothing is more disarming than showing a man that you value not only his mind, but also his opinions even of disagree. That tells me that it's okay for me to talk to you. That tells me that we're more just gotta relax and open your cars. Who knows, he may even enlighten you on some things that are worthwhile. All too often, your focus is to change us, which is not always a bad thing, but don't have intentions of change us, which is not always a bad thing, but don't have intentions of changing us and no intentions of even entertaining the thought of changing yourself (which I'll get into later). That's not fair. Relationships are all about compromising. Compromising means bending a little that may be outside of what's normal for you. The purpose of this is so that this thing that we have going on, it fits BOTH OF US, not just you.

Just like in the lying chapter, don't make it hard for us to have those conversations by, first being su-

Chapter 5 If He Shuts Down When the Convo Is Real

per argumentative, unruly, unwilling to compromise, and, most importantly, unwilling to listen and make adjustments when needed. The next time that you have something on your mind that you feel needs to be addressed, take a different approach. Early in the day, shoot him a text to the extent of the following: "Hey baby, I hope that you're having a good day. I want to go out tonight. It's been a while, and I think that we just need some one-on-one time to unwind. See you when you get home. I love you!"

What the text does is put him on point that you do have something planned for the two of you. That way, you don't have to worry about him getting off and going straight to the pool hall. Next, the approach of your text is real disarming. You're not being hostile. In fact, you should like a real loving person that has some damn sense.

Once you have calm and ease over dinner, you let him know, "Hey, there are somethings that I believe we both need to address as far as the relationship is concerned." The use of the words "we both" is so important because you're letting him know that you aren't here to tear him down. This isn't "destroying session". You're here to build and add on. The most important thing that you can do tonight is first be a good listener, even when you hear shit that you don't want to or that you even deem wrong, and next is, check your emotions. Remember, y'all are here to find some common ground, not to set the relationship back even further than it already is.

Trey wants this thing to work, ladies, he does, which is why he's still here. He has hopes that things will someday go back to what it once was. Meet him half-way.

Now let's look at Dion's side. From the very jump, Dion probably always have been elusive when it comes to these types of conversations. I'm talking since day one. Have you ever asked Dion what you mean to him? What's love to him? Ever asked him to simply tell you how he feels about you? If not, ask him. I would bet money if he says some dumb shit like," I mean, you cool. I love you!" Who in the fuck wants to hear that? You ask those questions because you want your lover to dig deep and really give you a scoop of his heart, and this person tells you some dumb shit like, "I mean, you cool. I love you!" I gotta secret though. The Dion's of the world, they run when it's real because of two reasons: (1) They are incapable of keeping it a stack (1,000 percent) with you, and (2), they know that enough "communication" about things of a serious nature, will ensure that they are found out. Under your microscope, it's only but so long that he can just freestyle (bullshit off the top of his head, no rehearsal) before he starts to sound like a broken record, in which you'll then know that you have been the only one taking this relationship seriously.

Despite the fact that he's slow, Dion's not retarded (and I don't say that often about anyone). He knows that he's not built to entertain these types of conversations, which is why when you go, he just looks at you without responding, allows you to pour your heart out, and will say something like, "... I feel you, I'll do better." You can approach him in the very same way I told you to take with Trey, and the results will not be the same. Remember, Trey wants this to work simply because he feels something for YOU. He wants to be with YOU. Nine times out of ten, Dion is not with you because of YOU. It's what you can do, are doing, or willing to do for him. Which always takes me back to parameters and boundaries. I will say in this in EVERY chapter and give you a different break-down every time. Ladies, it's a must that early on, you set these guidelines of what you're going to go for and not. Had those serious questions been asked early on (What's a relationship to you, how do you look at love, and what's your definition, As far as the relationship is considered, what's your goal?). A lot of times, y'all fail to even ask the simplest things that will give you an immediate heads-up. Things like, "What's your type? What qualities turn you on the most in a woman?". These things should be the ground floor because the answer to these questions will often tell you everything that you need to know. Once again, allow him to filter himself early so that you're not reading this book right now, trying to do it yourself. Hopefully, by this point, I still have your attention because I can promise you that it only gets better.

Chapter 6 If the Marriage Convo Is One that He Often Neglects

Still here! I'm glad you are because shit is really starting to heat up now. I think the aka for this chapter will be, the "action chapter". I say that because I'm going to stir up the type of emotions in this chapter that's going to make you go and get active. Dion just might find all his shit on the front porch after this one. Marriage is the highlight of this chapter.

Let's all say it together one time: MARRIAGE? Correct me if I'm wrong, marriage is the end game, right? To all the "girlfriends" out there, you do want to one day be a wife, right? Well, if not, this isn't the chapter for you. In fact, this isn't the book for you.

Right now, we're solely focusing on the wives-to-be. To all of the good ladies out there that's effectively holding the fort down and your man in the same breath, let me be the first to tell you that, YOU DESERVE A RING! That's Right. You're not the only one who felt this way, but let's address what's important to ensure that you get that ring.

Before we delve deep, answer me this first: Are you a RING MATERIAL? What makes you a RING MATERIAL? (Just like I say he should be able to answer certain questions, you should be able to give a definite answer to these two questions before anything else. Assuming that you're going to keep it a stack (1000 percent) and that you just gave me some of the best answers that I've ever heard, we now get down to the meat and potatoes.

Have you been doing this dance with Trey for a minute now, and it seems like y'all get no closer to tying the knot? Do you look at everyone around you and silently wonder how and why most of them are married or about to do it and not you? Does it piss you off every time you go on the Internet and see someone or another gloating about their recent engagement? Not because you're a hater but, being honest about it, because it's not you? Well lucky for you, you have me.

Ladies, the harsh reality of this thing with Trey is, he dodges the conversation or flat out stays away from it because he's unsure about making you his wife. He hasn't seen enough to make him confident enough to ensure that marrying you won't be the biggest mistake of his life. With everything that he already has to put up with and, everything that you have displayed thus far, let's be honest, you're not the perfect candidate, with all the crazy and selfish shit. I mean, if you were in his shoes, would you marry you? If not, why not? If so, why so? Really, I want you to take a moment to honestly answer those questions. Ladies, marriage for us means something totally different us than it does for y'all. For us, marriage means that the jersey is officially hung up (I can't play anymore), the Nike's are to be put up (I can't run anymore), and my nuts will officially be put on the freezer (no more loose ass). (I know it sounds crazy to hear it like that, but y'all know I've been keeping it a stack [1000 percent] since page one.) So, seeing how big of a decision that is for us, you have to understand that our filtering process is a meticulous one.

Marriage means that, for the rest of this thing that I call life, this woman right here will be my partner (Are you truly a PARTNER? Have you been that? Or have you been a DICTATOR?) I'm forever obligated to deal with her good and bad sides. Now, we hear the entire statement, but the word that speaks the loudest to us is her. "bad". All of that equates to this being the biggest decision of a man's life, so we hear forever, we equate that with a life sentence. No sane man is going to deliberately walk into hell when he doesn't have to. So when the convo is posed (if it comes up at all) and he's not as vocal as he should be or you'd like him to be, his silence is telling you everything that you need to know. This is one of those situations where, his lack of words tells you everything that you need to know.

We know when we got a good one. That's a fact because a good one makes you want to be better. So more than anything else, we want to slap the cuffs on her. When it's like that, you don't have to worry about bringing the convo to the forefront because he will, or, better yet, one day, you'll look down, and he'll be on his knee. But in order to get that ring, ladies, you have to be something that he can see himself with forever and not in a toxic manner.

Now usually, most of my enthusiasm comes in giving you the world according to Trey, but this topic has Dion written all over it. If you're dealing with Dion, the marriage convo is one that he often neglects because HE HAS NO PLANS IN MARRYING YOUR ASS! That's right, and I put it in small capital letters so that you can't miss it. Under no circumstances, unless you hit the lottery or some shit like that, is he willing to tie himself down to you and put his nuts in the freezer. That was never his goal. That never will be. Why will he put a shackle on himself when he has no plans of being with you for the long haul? I hate to be the bearer of bad news, but, ladies, there's a good chance that as soon as he finds something just a little better, he will leave you. Dion is a rolling stone and can't be kept, and any woman that thinks that she can keep him is delusional person that subconsciously likes to be hurt.

All of you with Dion's, can we be honest for a second? You know damn well that you don't have a chance at hell at marrying this man. With that being said, if marriage isn't the goal, what is he still around for? Damn, I hit one the time, right? To take it even further, why would you want to marry a character of such anyway? Don't you value yourself more than that? You should. The sad reality is, you don't and he knows that you don't. So he drags you whichever way he pleases.

Which takes me directly into, PARAMETERS AND BOUNDARIES. From the jump, ladies, it's imperative that you let it be known. "Hey, I'm looking for a husband and not just a good time." Off the bat, that lets us know, "Okay, sure, this is serious." That statement that you at, or draw me closer because what I'm looking for is a woman that knows exactly what she wants. I can't stress how important it is to COMMUNICATE these things early on because if we never have these conversations and I'm one of those guys that have no intentions of getting married, I'm going to have NO understanding when you wake up one day and are flipping about the topic at hand. Had you been a better COMMUNICATOR of the things that you really want from a man, Dion's ass wouldn't have ever made it through the door, and that's a fact because from the jump, you would've known that he was bullshit. For the most part, ladies, if you allow me to "play", that's exactly what I'm going to do, "play". If Dion, knows that he can reap all of the benefits of being with you (exclusivity, the key to your body, the key to your mind, somewhere to stay, someone that's going to put up with all of his shit and take him back time after time) without that type of commitment, why would he do it? Ever heard the saying, "Why buy the cow, when the milk is free"? Can I get a witness today?

 Parameters and boundaries, ladies, parameters and boundaries. Lighten up on Trey and work on yourself. If you can make necessary adjustments, I promise you, he will too. Dion, if you know like I know, you'll throw your bookmark in the spine of this book RIGHT NOW, and start packing all of his shit.

CHAPTER 7 IF HE TALKS TO YOU IN A DEMEANING MANNER

So it's gotten this far, huh? Every time he gets pissed now, he says something that makes you think, "Oh, he's got me fucked up," right? Does he occasionally hit below the belt and touch on issues that you're sensitive about, like your weight or those feet? Does he tell you things that stab at your self-confidence, like "Look at you, don't anybody want you?"

Verbal abuse is what they call it. Being in a place of love, peace, and serenity in my own life, by no means do I condone in any kind of abuse, verbal, emotional, or physical (especially physical), which is one of the big reasons that I'm making my contribution to women by way of giving you these gems, because seeing my own mother go through a lot of the same things that you are; to see her hurt on more than one occasion, left me with my own scars. But that's a subject for the last chapter. Ladies, if you relationship has reached this point, it's a must that you hit pause and re-evaluate EVERYTHING that's going on.

If Trey sporadically snaps out on you and goes below the belt 9 times out of 10, it's because he's fed up with everything that's transpired from chapters

1-6. Hurt people often hurt people. Never forget that. Ladies, some of you can get so stuck in your ways and have been one way for so long that, what's normal to you (boisterous, hot-tempered, inconsiderate, selfish, and BOUT DAT LIFE!) seems like a rite of passage when in reality, you're a very abusive person. Although we're thought to be different species than your very own self, in relation to being offended and verbally assaulted, it's only but so much we're going to take before we buck back.

I believe that to only be human nature. Being that we're men, society has created this false misconception that we're unshakable, emotionless, numb beings, which is completely false because at the beginning and end of every day, we're human beings first and foremost, and it stirs up emotion, as it should.

Trey will only be docile for so long before you get what you're getting now, and the crazy thing about it is, most of what he says that cuts deep is what he really feels. Now I'm not saying that this is his preferred method to let you know it, but at this moment, you're dealing with a man that has his back against the wall.

Something else that has to be understood is, ladies, we're driven by our pride and ego, even some of the best and highly evolved in the species. Even a man that is not controlled by those things, he's still side affected by those things. So, when those things start to be tinkered with, poked at, or scratched at, a whole other side of us comes out. This is the side that normally makes irrational decisions and has lapse in judgment, logic goes out of the window, and him speaking to you in this manner is the outcome.

It's not right, but what else can you expect? A law of nature says that 'like begets like' meaning that whatever you put out there, you will most likely get back in return. Take notice in how you're received when you walk into a room of people and you come in with positive energy and say, "How's everyone doing?" The positive energy that you entered this room with will mostly likely be met with the same type of energy. And this law really seems to stand strong when we're dealing with negative things. That negative force is so strong that it's imperative that you try your best to alleviate it at all costs. I think you're starting to catch my drift.

As we always do it around this time, let's now flip the focus to Dion. In addition to all of the other "burn-out" shit that you've been dealing with concerning this "person", he also has the nerve to come out of his mouth and demean you, and put you down. This is after you put up with an array of bullshit and take care of him like I do. I know your question is, "How can he find it in himself to talk to me in this way?" If you aren't asking this question, I don't know why you aren't. To you, queen I wish that I could get face-to-face with you so that you could hear the conviction in my voice and see the sincereness in my eyes when I tell you that, he talks down to you and demean you because to him, you're beneath him. He doesn't see you as his equal (which I'll go in depth in the following chapter). You're nothing of value to him. Whereas Trey's words we're rooted in some type of pain that was firstly imposed on him, Dion's words are formed from a general lack of respect and mechanism of controlling you. Ladies, when a man has little-to-no respect for you, he will treat you any kind of way and talk to you in the same manner without ever being provoked. This is commonly used as a control mechanism. When he knows that his verbal abuse has a tremendous effect on you, it will be continually used to "keep you in check" and off-balanced.

I stress the off-balance part because a focused mind, one that is on balance, can't be shaken. It can't be controlled. On the contrary, the unbalanced mind is a mind that can't focus. You're incapable of seeing things as they truly are, making you susceptible to his control mechanism. A man like Dion will use certain methods to break a woman and make her into a "floormat" (something that is laid down with NO RESISTANCE). These methods are similar to the antebellum (times before the Civil War) days when the White people put certain tactics into play to turn a potentially rebelling human being into a docile slave. Everything first starts at the mind, and nothing wreaks havoc on the mind like verbal abuse. It makes you depressed. You feel less than, and will even start to buy into the bullshit that he says, slowly transforming yourself from a queen into whatever he's now telling you that you are. There is no love that will allow a man to do this to you.

No man that loves you will have you believe that you're stupid. No, a man that loves a woman, that isn't up to par mentally, will help and protect that woman. No man that loves you will have you believe that you're not worth anything. On the contrary, he'll

CHAPTER 7 IF HE TALKS TO YOU IN A DEMEANING MANNER

SHOW you that you're worth everything. No man that loves you will make you feel as if what you say doesn't matter. Your true love will make it his business to make it known that you're heard and that your opinion counts. A commonly used smoke screen that Dion often uses is, after tearing you down, he might follow up with a show of gratitude, flowers, a few nice words here and there, or some crazy-ass sex where, in the midst of it, he whispers in your ear, "I love you". This is never genuine, EVER! This is to keep you under his spell, the spell that you've been under for so long that you can't seem to shake off of yourself. Don't be fooled by this! If his shit wasn't on the porch by the end of this last chapter, there's no reason that it isn't now. As you can clearly see, Trey and Dion have two completely different approaches to this negativity. Trey's is a response; Dion's is a tactic.

Which brings me back to PARAMETERS AND BOUNDRIES. From the jump, ladies, it's a must that, in addition to you keeping your own cool and being toxic, negative, and nasty, you COMMUNICATE that you will not be accepting such behavior either. There's a big difference between a heated conversation and being disrespected. At times, we all can use a small "check" so to speak, but it should never be anything to send you into a depression. That's not love. That's hurt. Our mouths were intended for loving. That's why a kiss feels so good, and so does oral... damn, I strayed for a second!

Words are powerful and can literally build or destroy. Instead of destroying the person that you claim to love and the relationship in the process, use your mouth for praises and, blessing, and for EFFECTIVELY COMMUNICATION. I promise, it'll work.

Chapter 8 Doesn't Treat You as an Equal

Ladies, I can only imagine that at this point, your spirit is all but broken, your confidence is shot, and you've probably started feeling like you might as well accept what Dion has to dish out, because this is about the best you're going to get, right?

If this is the case, Dion has won. He's defeated you. He has broken your spirits and hypnotized you to where, if you look in the mirror and really evaluate yourself, you'll see that you're a shell of who you used to be and none of the woman that you're supposed to be.

Let's rewind and pinpoint exactly where all of this took place. He started out as someone that was cool, has a little swag, and made you laugh. You gave him some ass and his sex was decent enough to keep you content. You allowed him to move in, and that where things started to change. You started to notice a LOT OF unfavorable behavior, like the lies that started to mount up and reveal that he was a lying piece of shit. The lying turned into staying out late and cheating, which, for some strange reason, you overlooked. By this time, Dion knows that he has you on the hook, so this is where his warfare starts to be aimed at your mind. The way that he speaks to you now, is in a demeaning manner; belittles you, and tears you down from the top up. And all of this is a result of him not seeing you as an equal, plain and simple. Now I want you to brace yourself, because the wound that you've just put a band aid on, I'm about to rip it off. It may hurt, but I promise it's for the best,

Ladies, him not seeing you, or treating you as an equal, is 100% YOUR FAULT.

Wait, wait, wait; before you curse me out, tell me, FUCK YOU, and close this book, hear me out. To be treated as an equal simply means that the manner in which I treat you will be nothing different than I treat myself. Period! Dion doesn't see you this way; which is why he has resorted to exploitation, control, and brainwashing you into believing all the things that you now believe about yourself.

Underestimating him and not taking care of your business early on has gotten you into a world of trouble, and now it's all bad. The worst part about it is, he knows exactly how much of a hold that he has over you, which allows him to be more reckless than ever, more disrespectful than ever, more cold and calloused and unloving than anyone that you've ever been with.

Ladies, if it's to the point where; when he does hurtful things, it no longer hurts, it's not because it's not that bad; it's because he's done so much to you, taken you through so much that you've become desensitized to the pain. Quick question, the last time you caught him cheating, did it hurt you like it used to?

Did you cry about it like you used too? See what I mean? At what point does pain not be pain anymore? Anyone? Anybody? Please allow me. Pain stops being pain, when you're used to it, and to have gotten used to negative pain is a clear sign that your faculties have been rearranged. Coming to this realization and finally holding the mirror up in a way that you never have, you're probably asking yourself now, "HOW did I get here?" right? Settling, settling for NOTHING. Settling for the sake of "not being alone", is what has you in the face that you're in right now.

I once heard a song called "After the Pain", by Betty Wright, and she says in the song,

"I've realized that having a piece of a man is better than having no man at all". When I heard it, all I could say was, Dion, no lie! I had to play this song for about an hour, just make sure what that quoted lyric was - listening intently to EVERY WORD that this magnificent artist sang to me - and I couldn't have disagreed more.

All correct. I could think, why in the hell she wanted a piece of a man; a piece! To agree with that, is to say: "what you do to me and say to me, I will not leave you simply because I do not want to be alone, and to have a trash ass man by my side, and is better than not having any man at all". This is what you're telling yourself. I don't know you personally, but I will almost bet it all on the fact that, you're worth more than that.

You're worth love; worth a smile; you're worth all the affection. You're worth the most in confidence; you're worth self-worth. You're worth nights where you can sleep good and days where you stay home to be loved down by someone that truly feels that way about you. You're worth the ring, the cake, and the dress. You're worth a solid man; with solid intentions; that only wants to assist you in becoming the absolute best version of yourself. You're worth an explanation. You're worth everything that he's made you believe that you aren't worthy of.

And I know this because, in my heart, I feel that "EVERY" woman is worth these same exact things.

Now, I will say, some women are not in the shape to receive those things at this very moment, but at the core, just being a woman, it's your God given right to be worthy of these things. But by now we all know, or should know, where all of the good things are magic and all of the crazy shit is not. Let's say it ether matters or it don't.

My man, Yo Gotti, said it best on his song, "Respect you earn - Ladies, what you make me do, is what I'm going to do". If you fail to set the standard, he will set one, and the one that he sets might not be intended in your favor. From the jump, please know that you set the table, just pick up what you put down, and move out accordingly. It's imperative that you let us know from the jump that you will be treated no less than what you're worth.

When he slips and is getting off course, don't overlook that. Don t make excuses for that. Don't compromise your core values, because this will surely lead you having the exact problem of not being treated as equal. The way I look at it is, it's hard to lose when you re the one that has made the rules. That's the focus right now, winning the relationship game. Set the bar, and set it high in regard to your worth.

If you've paid attention, you've noticed that every chapter before now, has started with me giving you this relationship from the perspective of 'Trey and casually worked my way to Dion. For this number here, I took a different approach and gave you Dion first. That wasn't by chance or mistake, because ladies, if you have a Trey, at his worst, Trey still sees you as his equal and treats you as such, in his own little way.

Granted, I know that he hasn't been the ideal lover, and has done some ill advised things, but most of his actions are motivated by things that you do (or don't).

Unlike Dion, Trey has no intentions of tricking you to be what he needs. He just hopes that it can/will take place organically, as it should. For the ladies with a Trey, I know that you may question his love sometimes; question his actions, in relation to the love that he's proclaimed, tight' From me to you, contrary to what it may look like, he really does love you; feels exactly what he tells you he does. It's your self-sabotaging behavior that throws the relationship out of whack. The fact that you come with an abundance of your own extras, you make it hard to love you like he really wants to, but he does love you.

Nevertheless. (as I'm writing this, I'm aware of exactly how it sounds, but we men are wired different.) I mean, let's be honest. Would a man that didn't love your ass, put up with the bullshit that you come with? The accusations, the verbal abuse, the distrust, the resistance, and all of the other self-sabotaging shit that you have going on? Trust me when I say, it will be a lot easier to just leave you and start anew, but something in you that shines so bright, at times, that it gives him hope. The love that he harbors for you, gives him hope. Hope that, with time, you'd come around and be for him what you once was, be what he needs you to be what you potentially could be.

The ways of a Trey may never be understood by you. You may feel that he's always looking for an excuse to fuck up, fuck off, or to go and do some dumb shit, but that is not true at all. The truth is that you push him into these unfavorable situations with your self-sabotaging behavior (which I will define in the final chapter). Ladies, if you have a Trey, it's time to tighten up and make things tight. If you have a Dion, it's time to tighten up and shake that dead weight.

Chapter 9 If He Hits You – Run!

I can only hope that this is the chapter that applies to the least of you. I hope that none of you are going through this shit. Verbal abuse is one thing, and, in a lot of cases, is the worst of abuse, but even with that being said, it doesn't diminish how bad being physically hurt really is. Ladies, this right here is Dion at his finest. I mean just look at all of the other behaviors that preceded this. You could see it coming. And not to mislead, I want to be clear ALL ABUSE IS PHYSICAL ABUSE. I want to make it crystal clear that isn't what I'm saying, but for the most part you catch my drift. Through my own travels as a man, I've learned that, due to a lack of knowing how to EFFECTIVELY COMMUNICATE, one will often impose on you, his will, to your opinions on you, by way of physicality. Did you lust see what happened? I said; due to a lack of knowing how to, one will often fly to impose his will or opinions on you by way of physicality. Do you see how what we started this off with (communication) has come back full circle. As with most of his other actions, Dion needs little to no provocation, to put his hands on you and will often sum it up by telling you that you made him do it, or that it was your fault that it happened to you. The worst thing that you can do is ever buy into that trash.

Ladies, I don't care what you do, don't care what you say: NO MAN has the right to physically chastise you.

And no real one will even attempt it. The action of fighting a woman comes from deep insecurities, inner weakness. When he acts out on you like this, this is him putting his weaknesses and vulnerabilities on full display. Getting personal for a second, coming up, I saw a lot of this with my own mother. I saw the same guys that swore that they loved her to death, be willing to beat her to death. I also remember seeing her take these same trash–ass guys back time after time.

I remember first feeling helpless, just being a child, witness to it all.

Then I remember feeling angry because she'd always take them back. My anger was rooted in the fact that, I had absolutely no understanding of why/how you wanted to still be with someone after they showed you that they were capable of only hurting you. I also didn't understand that my mother was broken. I didn't realize that she'd put so much into these trash–ass men, that it had taken too much out of her to be able to see things clearly. I didn't understand that she didn't t value herself, as I did. This not only made her-not-only accept this behavior and treatment, but she also made excuses for it at times. It took my mother YEARS to shake these deficiencies, but with TIME, she did. I stress here because when you look at the years 3-years put into that Dion, and years spent on another Dion, by the time you look up, you've given fourteen years of yourself to Dion and have nothing but bad memories and wounds to show for it. Was/is it worth it?

I'm a firm believer that, just like your mouth, your hands were made for loving, holding, caressing, and to make you feel secure, rub, and touch: NOT TO BEAT AND MANGLE.

Just like anything else though, it's easy to get desensitized to it, due to the frequency that its happened, or even the frequency that we've seen it occur. When you find yourself saying shit like:

"Oh, it doesn't happen all of the time, only gets crazy when he's drunk and that one was my fault"!

There is a serious problem that you need to address immediately. You've become so brainwashed and confused that you think that it's okay if a man loses his control to the point where he's liable to go upside your head. Who in the hell wants to always have to be on alert for a swift jab or cross from the person that claims they love you? Even when he drunk, who wants to have to worry about him putting your head through a wall?

There's nothing to justify this ladies which takes me to the most consistent part of my philosophy, PARAMETERS AND BOUNDARIES. Just as with everything else, ladies, it's a must that you set the standard of what this relationship will and won't entail. It's a must that you check his ass at the very first sign of aggression, and at the very first time that he tries it, you terminate the contract. Just like I did for the last chapter, I saved Trey for the end. Simply put this isn't Trey at all. He's had his fair share of mishaps, but when it comes to hurting you, physically, he loves you too much, values you too much, or is just morally sound enough to never allow himself to do any sucker shit as such.

On the contrary, you may be the one losing your cool and imposing your shit will on him at times. I really hope that this is not the case - THAT shit no man wants hit on and scratched up. The shit is in the way IMBARRASSING! When you see a man walkin' around and he has scratches all on his neck and face, the world knows that "'his woman has went crazy to his ass".

Ladies, this that is not cute nor acceptable. Regardless of how pissed off you are about something or another, you getting physical is not the solution. In fact, the only thing that this is going to do is make him lie and for sure cheat with someone that isn't going to go to his ass, really stay out late, and further delay the ring. And depending on how tired of this shit he is, you may need a lawyer and bond money. Domestic violence goes both ways. You do know that, right'? Okay just making sure that were all on the same page.

Inclosing this chapter, I want to stress that; no man and NOTHING that he has to offer, is worth him puttin his hands on you. Fuck all that - "I'm sorry baby, I was drunk; Please don't leave me; I need you", and bullshit promises. That's always gonna follow, and I promise you that it's going to sound super sincere, sound just like some shit that you're supposed to believe, some—shit that you're supposed to believe, but DO NOT FOOL YOURSELF. He has tricked YOU in every other way NOT allow him to convince you that this shit is cool - because it's not.

Ladies, if he hits you, RUN fast can and never look back!

Chapter 10 The Solution

We've made it. If you made it this far without throwing this book in the trash, I salute you. I salute you for listening to me, even when you didn't agree, and trusting me enough to keep going with the mind frame that this last chapter was going to give you all of the clarity that you need.

By now, you know exactly what you have. It's either a Trey; "Ain't Shit, but Can Be Saved" or a Dion - "Ain't Shit and Ain't Gonna Be".

Which resolves the first step for us, pinpointing the character. Now that he's recognized, and has a name, we now figure out how to go about it all.

To all of my ladies dealing with a Dion: call me straight to the point. That if you haven t packed up all of his shit yet, I must ask why? What are you waiting for? Do you have hopes that he will be any different than what I just told you? If this is the case you've just wasted a couple of dollars because true change isn t what you want at all. After all that you've been through with this person and as much time as you ye wasted, when will you ever get the confidence to what you know you should've done a long time ago? JUST DO IT - Sack that shit right now! Don t even think about it just get active. Don t talk about shit - look him in the face, don't respond to his text or calls, in fact, change your number; the same time that you change your locks. He's not worth your time AT ALL. It's time for yourself and it's time to rebuild and I'm gonna to tell u how to do just that.

To all of my ladies dealing with a Trey, putting your stubbornness to the side, you must feel some type of way to read about how crazy you've been acting, is a lot different than hearing it from him isn t it (and I don't even know you) or so you think I know your character all too well, because I was Trey. I was that good guy that was led to do stupid things because of a lack of this or too much of that; or the unwillingness to compromise.

I personally know what its like to love someone that makes me do shit, to whereas my actions aren't matching my words. I know, I know, go ahead and say it; I know for a fact that you're saying, l don t make you do shit. You do what you want to do. You lie to me because you want to. You talk to other women because you want to. I know you're saying it and as much as you may not want to take accountability for my shortcomings in this relationship, you played a role. Put your pride to the side and continue to walk with me. You're a very strong and passionate woman with qualities that a man like myself loves, but those same qualities can and have been your undoing. But, just like I told all of my ladies that are dealing with the Dions, it s time to get yourself together and a time to rebuild.

Chapter 10 The Solution

The first step to rebuilding is to acknowledge the fact that CHANGE needs to take place. Do you want better results or do you want more happiness and less toxicity? Do you want a true partner? Well, it's time to change, ladies. To change is usually marked by the feeling of finally being tired. In this instance, were talking about tired of failure. All to, often, I hear people say that they're tired of that; tired of that, but then they go right back to the same shit that they just said they were tired of - with no intentions of doing anything differently. If this is you, I understand that you're not tired , you just like to complain.

When you're tired, you make a change in that action that you're tired of, immediately ! Let's think about a person that just worked an 8 hour shift. When he says, "Man, I'm tired"," there ain't gonna be any partying, kicking it, dancing, painting, sex, nothing. As soon as he can, he's going to Iye down and go to sleep. He's going to physically shut his body down and no longer do anything to contribute to him being tired.

Let's take another. You -'ye been running for about a mile now fatigue is starting to set in. As soon as you get to that point where you say; "Damn, I'm tired". What are you going to do next? You're going to stop immediately. See how tired people operate? They don t complain of fatigue and fail to address the problem. Which is what brings me to you. If you spent your own good money on this fantastic work out, that s a sign that you're tired and looking for answers. The next step is vowing to get active today.

Are u and I really ready for a relationship? This question is so amazing and too often ignored. A lot of times, we as human neglect our true needs for minor wants, and it ends up setting us back and makes us pay for it every time. At some point, as an adult, we have to stop running from the person in the mirror and deal with him/her before we can constructively deal with anybody else. What sense does it make for me to help you get your business off the ground and when my own is in trouble of failure? We do this, and do it often. A lot of times, past situations and relationships leave us with so much trauma and residue, that we never address. II sweep it under the rug as (that shit didn't t affect us) and it has it's way of showing up on Trey and manifest in the form of self-sabotaging behavior.

How this is often done in the name of not being alone, a lot of times, but let me ask you this 'what's wrong with being alone? The person that rebels at being alone for any amount of time is a person that doesn't t want to deal with the shit that they're supposed to be dealing with. It's easy to distract yourself when you have the company of someone else, and that's never good. Ladies, it's a must that before you can expect a man to deal with you.

You first deal with self because the neglect that you show yourself is what gives birth to all of the negative behavior and your insecurities. These negative emotions that make you suspect him a fighting enhance. It's important that you realize what type of trauma your last relationship has left you with. It's important ON: This sounds confusing, that you recognize exactly how broken you may be, because when you acknowledge that you have a problem for clarity, you're more prone to correcting those problems you see. As humans, it's innate in our nature to not be alone. It's a natural feeling. We are meant to be social beings, but remember, were not just talking about having a relationship here. We're looking for quality relationships. We're shooting for success in our relationships. At the end of every day, just make sure that you're taking care of self before anything else.

   Now that you have definitively made the decision to get active and make that change and go into rebuild mode; you must pull out the scale and value yourself. You can NEVER expect someone to see in you; what you don't first see in yourself.

   Amongst the first questions you should be asking yourself, now that we're not running away from the woman in the mirror is, "What do I bring to the table? Am I an asset or a liability? If I am an asset, what makes me that (it should be more than your pretty face and nice body)? If I'm a liability, what do I need to work on? I can't stress the importance of communication enough, but it doesn't just travel both ways; at times you have to effectively communicate with your own self. Once you can get to the point where you can be completely honest with yourself about these things, you know that we've made progress. In the event that your answers are not really to your liking, don't get depressed. Don't get down on yourself; no need for that! All that means that now we have something to work on. We have some work to do. It may be going to get you a job, because for so long, you've been allowing him to take care of you. It may be upgrading from the job and opening the business that you've always wanted, to give you more control over your life. It may be counseling, to address some things that you've been trying to suppress. Whatever it is, the accumulation of it should make you a better version of yourself. This part of the rebuild is critical because your self-worth is going to be your foundation, your solid ground. Yourself worth is going to dictate how you move from this point on, and what you allow into your circle.

Stay Fly. This right here is a big part of your "shake back". It is all part of the process to get your "shake back". As we all know, when you look good, you feel good. When you feel good, you do better. Stress and depression has a way of deteriorating you from the inside out. It starts with wreaking havoc on your mind than your physical. You may have gained weight, lost, weight, and your flair for being on top of your game, like you once was. It's time to get back to that. As we all know, appearance is everything, and a lot of times, just like your reputation, it precedes you. With that being said and known, it's time to put it all back together. If you're big on the details, take you a day out and start getting your nails done again. Spend a few dollars on yourself, and go get you some new gear and new kicks. Get the wig done. Hold on though, we aren't finished yet.

We're reintroducing an entire new lifestyle. Get that body right; this part may be long overdue. Do you often compare yourself to the old you? Do you look in the mirror and not like what you see now? No problem; am I tripping on that because we're getting active from this point on. Switch up your diet. I'm not saying starve or go keto or sonic or other extreme shit, but switch it up. Eliminate the beef and pork or at least cut down on it. Incorporate fruits into your every day now. Instead of the fries, get you a salad sometimes.

This is the "'shake back" because like I said, "when you look good, you feel good, and when you feel good, you do better". Hit that gym or hit the track, or even your living room floor, in an effort to lose whatever is unwanted, or to just tone up. NO ONE CAN DO THIS, IT'S FOR YOU.

You will never be complete if your BODY and SPIRIT aren't in sync. Ladies, this is a celebration, a celebration of eliminating what it once was, and what it's about to be. Men LOVE, LOVE, LOVE a fly ass woman. Confidence attracts. Get you a routine and stick to it, that's the life. Set your standards and stand on that. Now it's time to erase any thing that once was. However, you use to move, it's time to dry erase, get used to an empty canvas and construct something else.

Ladies this is where we're setting those PARAMETERS and BOUNDARIES. What are you focused on? What will you absolutely not deal with? What's the absolute deal breaker? This sounds incoherent, kind of a breaker for you; and why? (why is this question so important for you to answer, because when you have rephrase for clarity, a definitive reason for why you can't deal with something, you're more prone to stick to the script).

What are the "must haves", and why? This is another important factor because it's seen as a critical part of the filtering process. For example, if it's a must have, that he has his two front teeth, then you meet those dudes back-to-back, and they're all bald mouth, you don't even have to go through the process of getting to know them, or even give them the chance to get to know you, because this was already something that was a mandatory (although I hope that you don t base your criteria solely on looks).

As far as success in the relationship arena, we must focus on the essentials first, and then allow the 'look based elements' to compliment those things, not the other way around. When we speak on essentials to be more specific were talking about other things, like COMMUNICATION - you knew that I was goin there where you talk to him with versatile conversation.

Dion has values and morals that mean the most to him. What does he believe and what does he stand on? Does he move in accordance with what he says he believes? Is he someone everything, and more often than not, jump the gun on.

Trey, do your insecurities make it virtually impossible to trust what is already established. If not, does he have that ambition and passion to get it? In my opinion I think that this is a must.

What do I know? I'm just the man who wrote the book giving you the game on rephrase for clarity.

And you may be thinking like, "Damn, these questions alone will make a man run", but trust me, if he's the one or has the potential, not only will he answer, he'll be elated to answer. I call this taking him to school, because in the event that you ask something that can't be answered, he'II treat it like homework and get back to you (at least, an interested one will). Usually through ones ambition and drive, you can normally tell if he's the leader type or not.

And there is a difference between a leader and a dictator. A leader is in to help realize the best and going to help you see you at your fullest potential.

A dictator is going to make you be what he wants you to be. No ifs, ands or buts about it. Does he make you feel good? This is a big part that can overshadow everything else but is very much needed to sustain.

And lastly, is he fly?

Yeah, I know this is essential but damn, we all appreciate something decent to look at? Speak for yourself, I know I do! Mother thing that should be looked at: does he have kids? If he does, do he take good care of them? What is the relationship with her and his kids mothers? This is another area that will tell you how he is built.

If he has kids that he doesn't take care of and spend time with, how much value can he really bring you? This should tell you that he's someone that doesn't take care of his business.

Now I want to make sure that I touch on the fact that, in the event that he isn't as involved as he should be, is it because the mother makes it hard for him to do?

Ladies you know how vindictive some women can be. They will use the child as a bargaining chip. If this is the case, then what I said doesn't apply. What s the relationship with them and the mother(s)? Ladies, I know that it intimidates some of you for a man to not be at odds with his child's mother, but the fact that he has a working relationship with her should be music to your ears.

This is a good sign that neither he nor she may be toxic. Just because they are on good terms doesn't t mean that she is someone that you will have to worry about. They would probably be together if they wanted each other.

Moving on, set those standards (you don't, he will, and if he does, there's not a guarantee that they will play in your favor!

When you set it, stand on it! The definition of this is simple, going against all of the standards that you just set. For the sake of the shake back, please don t abuse and disrespect the process by settling and accepting something below what you re worth. I know that stability is a big thing; and that we all, may certainly agree, have this nightmare fear of being alone.

Let me be the first to tell you that, the moment you settle, you rob yourself of true happiness and love in its purest. I know that you may be saying, "How long am I supposed to wait"? I'm lonely now. What you have to understand is that, everything doesn't happen on your time. We have a culture that's so accustomed to instant gratification, which lowers our threshold for patience. In the case of success in the relationship department, patience is the key. You in a rush to be shacked up, boned up and half assed wifed up- will have you reading this book over again in a year. See, rushing the process will make you omit certain things and will make you overlook certain things, telling yourself, "That's just one of those things and nobody's perfect. The perfect part is true, but when you factor in that your list wasn't that extensive and unrealistic, the man for you would've checked all of your boxes. The motto that I live by is as long as I do everything that's required of me –everything that happens for me will happen for me. This keeps me in a clear headspace and allows me to allow every process in my life, to fully mature and usher itself in my life. All I get is results, and there is no doubt that the same won't be true for you. Stand firm and never settle.

   Vacancies: This is a topic that's part of the process, but at the same time, it's what I call one of those outskirt elements. You need to hear this through. I told you that I was going to make sure that I equipped you with EVERYTHING that you would to need to be successful your first true relationship. I once heard that when you have no vacancies in your life, it's impossible for anyone new to be ushered in. When I first heard it, it was one of those things that went in one ear and out of the other, until people started falling out of my life. Just like you, I once had a fear of the unknown. I also thought like "Damn all that". Loosing all the time - where I was a soldier and when I was fucking up; but what I slowly started to realize was, the universe is forever working and really works for the person that's going with the flow. I noticed that every time I lost someone, they were replaced with someone of equal or greater value. At first I thought that I just lucked out - that was when I saw time after time after time, I knew definitively that this was the way. A lot of times, we tend to try to hold on to things or people that don't want to be held on to. We are in are fatiguing ourselves, when the right thing to do, is allow those things to do what it is that they really want to do. I know that it may be tough to do, hard even. I know that it's a good chance that it will hurt (if the love was real, it's inevitable that it hurt U) but as long as you keep living, it will be a defining moment in your life. We often act as if there's a shortage of people in the world, but the universe will see to it that as long as you have a vacancy, you will get what you need. It may be something new or it may be something old that made some adjustments and fine tuning.

All in all, you need that space. I know that you probably thought that it'll never end but we ye finally reached the checkered flags. What I've just given you is worth gold to the woman who's ready, and not even worth the paper it's printed on, to the woman whose not. This solution section has given you an excellent road map to putting an end to the negativity and a fresh start on doing it the way that it's supposed to be done. I strongly advise that if you're the woman that's coming off a Dion, to-give yourself at least a year of time to yourself, where you're implementing the process of the "shake back". This time spent correctly will be one of the best investments of time that you could ever make. A year removed and spent constructively, I promise you results.

To all of my ladies that's dealing with a Trey, take it easy. Please understand that you are your own worst enemy and your ways of self-sabotage must stop in order for you to have a successful relationship. It is defined here as conduct thought of to be precautionary to an inevitable end. To put in your mind thinking the worst, you often jump the gun, causing you to introduce negative elements (insecurity, verbal abuse, unwarranted suspicion, violence, and all types of foolishness) into the relationship, making it hard for one to love you to the full capacity. Unconsciously, you seek to terminate the relationship on your own terms, so that it won't depend on his. You're thinking like, "How did I do this". As bad as this may sound, it feels worse when you're the recipient of this behavior. I know firsthand. It's understood that your past traumas have left you with scars that you still see scars that remind you of times where you were used, abused, taken advantage of. Don't allow that to stop what could potentially be a good thing. If he s your king, trust him, love him and do better for him, because remember, he needs you as much as you need him.

To every set of eyes devouring these words right now, I hope that you use this method because not only am I guaranteeing you just a relationship! But I'm guaranteeing you a 'SUCCESSFUL ONE. I wish you success on every relationship that's a result of this work. As a man that s played the game from a few different positions in an attempt to find my own self, I've given you what I'ld give to my very own mother, daughter, or sister that a come as a result of my own travels. I not only put this together for women looking to better their situation, but also did it for the Treys that aren't always understood or know how to make what they feel to be understood in the ways that it needs to, without being taken as a cop–out or excuse.

Just as much as I want that success for the ladies, I want the same for the fellas. Its time for us to give birth to a new culture of effective communication and I m putting my best foot forward. I don t have all of the answers, but I speak on what I know definitively, as you should. I ask you to stay focused and vigilant, and strive for the very best of what this life has to offer you. I thank you for allowing my contribution to the world to enter your hands and penetrate your minds with thoughts that I can help heal your heart. With peace and blessings, I sign out.

Sincerely yours,
The Mindset aka Dontaz Wilkerson.

Printed by Libri Plureos GmbH in Hamburg, Germany